W9-ANB-135

Published in 2014 by The Rosen Publishing Group, Inc.
29 East 21st Street, New York, NY 10010

Photo Credits: **KEY** tl=top left; tc=top center; tcr=top center right; tr=top right; cl=center left; c=center; cr=center right; b=bottom; bl=bottom left; bcl=bottom center left; bc=bottom center; bcr=bottom center right; br=bottom right; bg=background

AAP = AAP Images; CBT = Corbis; GI = Getty Images; iS = istockphoto.com; PDCD = PhotoDisc; SH = Shutterstock; TF = Topfoto; TPL = photolibrary.com

front cover bl iS; **back cover** bc CBT; cl GI; **1**c TF; **2–3**bg iS; **4–5**bg TPL; **6–7**bg iS; **7**tl CBT; **8**bl CBT; **8–9**bg iS; tc TPL; **9**bl SH; br TF; cr iS; **10**br, tc CBT; bc, cl iS; tc TF; **10–11**bg SH; **11**bl TF; tc, tr CBT; **12**tl PDCD; **12–13**tc SH; **13**bg GI; **16–17**bg SH; **17**c GI; bc CBT; tc SH; **18**bl TF; tr SH; **18–19**tc SH; **19**bl CBT; br TF; **20**bl GI; tl AAP; **21–22**bg GI; **22**c, cbr, tl SH; tcr iS; **23**c, bg CBT; bcl, tl iS; **24**bc, bcl, tcl iS; **24–25**bg iS; **25**bc, bcr, tcr, tr, tl iS; **26–27**bg iS; **27**br, cr iS; tc CBT; **28**bl, br, cl, cr iS; **29**bl, br, cl, cr, tl, tr iS; **30**tr SH

All illustrations copyright Weldon Owen Pty Ltd. **14–15**c, **32**bg Dave Tracey

Weldon Owen Pty Ltd
Managing Director: Kay Scarlett
Creative Director: Sue Burk
Publisher: Helen Bateman
Senior Vice President, International Sales: Stuart Laurence
Vice President Sales North America: Ellen Towell
Administration Manager, International Sales: Kristine Ravn

Library of Congress Cataloging-in-Publication Data

McAllan, Kate.
 Urban habitats / by Kate McAllan.
     pages cm. — (Discovery education: Habitats)
 Includes index.
 ISBN 978-1-4777-1327-3 (library binding) — ISBN 978-1-4777-1489-8 (paperback) — ISBN 978-1-4777-1490-4 (6-pack)
 1. Urban ecology—Juvenile literature. 2. City and town life—Juvenile literature. I. Title.
 QH541.5.C6M29 2014
 577.5'6—dc23

                                  2012043615

Manufactured in the United States of America

CPSIA Compliance Information: Batch #S13PK3: For Further Information contact Rosen Publishing, New York, New York at 1-800-237-9932

URBAN HABITATS

KATE MCALLAN

PowerKiDS press.

New York

Contents

What Is a City?

People live in settlements of different sizes. Some live in dwellings that stand by themselves. Others live together in small settlements, such as villages, or in bigger ones, such as towns. Cities are the largest of all. Although cities can be crowded, noisy, hectic, and stressful, city life can also be exciting and interesting.

Harborside

The city of Hong Kong, China, is built on Victoria Harbor. Hong Kong is one of the world's most important trade and financial centers.

Cities are centers for trade, the arts, education, religion, and government. They have complex transportation, communication, waste, and water systems.

HOW BIG?

Different population figures are often given for the same city. Sometimes only people living in the city center are counted, and sometimes people in the outskirts are counted too. In 2009, the city of Tokyo, in Japan, was the world's most populous city, with 37 million living in its greater metropolitan area.

A busy shopping street in Tokyo

Lost Cities

Early cities developed where farmers could grow more than enough crops to feed themselves. This surplus supported people who focused on nonfarming activities, such as craft, building, and trade. Ancient cities were often fortified. They had large buildings, such as temples and palaces. Around the cities were road networks and irrigation systems. If food or other resources could no longer be supplied, cities collapsed.

The palace at Knossos, Crete
The Minoan palace at Knossos was the home of Crete's rulers. Between 1900 and 1400 BC, Knossos was a trade center for olive oil, perfume, cloth, and pottery. It shrank after a devastating earthquake around 1500 BC.

Teotihuacán, Mexico

Teotihuacán was the largest city in Mesoamerica between the first and eighth centuries. In about AD 700, the city's temples, palaces, and largest homes were burned. Some researchers believe an uprising against the city's ruling class caused its downfall.

Teotihuacán pyramid

The stepped pyramid at Teotihuacán was once covered in plaster and painted with bright murals. No one knows which god it was built to honor.

Angkor Wat, Cambodia

Angkor Wat was one of many temples in the city of Angkor, which existed in Cambodia from the ninth to fifteenth centuries. Debris from severe flooding may have choked the irrigation systems, leading to the city's downfall.

The Great Ziggurat of Ur, Iraq

The Great Ziggurat was the largest temple in the city of Ur, which thrived from about 2600 to 500 BC in what is now known as Iraq. The city collapsed when the climate became drier and irrigation systems failed.

A City Survives

Some cities that were founded long ago have continued to grow and meet the challenges of a changing world. In AD 43 the Romans invaded Britain. They built a fort on the River Thames and called it Londinium. Despite many ups and downs, this settlement has grown to be one of the largest cities in the world: London.

AD 60
Roman Londinium is destroyed by British queen, Boudica, but is rebuilt. In AD 410, the Romans leave and the city falls to ruin.

AD 886
The city has grown into a port ruled by King Alfred the Great. The Anglo-Saxons rebuild the Roman walls to defend against Vikings.

1066
After the Battle of Hastings, William the Conqueror is crowned king. London becomes a major political center in medieval Europe.

1348
The Black Death, a deadly bubonic plague that spread all over Europe, strikes London for the first time, killing half of its 80,000 people.

1665–1666
The Great Plague kills 70,000 people. It only vanishes when the Great Fire destroys four-fifths of the city.

1858
The stench of the heavily polluted River Thames leads to funding for an improved sewerage system.

1940
The German bombings during World War II force thousands to sleep in underground tube stations.

1952
Heavy fog mixed with deadly pollution leads to the first Clean Air Act being introduced.

2003
The Congestion Charge for drivers is introduced to encourage greater use of public transportation.

Paris, France
The capital of France is famous for its cafés, fashion, art, and beautiful buildings. Notre Dame, its main cathedral, stands on the island in the Seine river where Paris was founded.

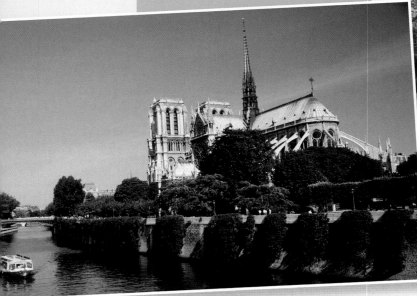

Shanghai, China
The old part of Shanghai has narrow streets. Many European-style buildings are in the old trade area. The Pudong New Area is a modern industrial zone with factories and apartment buildings.

Modern Cities

To operate successfully, cities must have infrastructure, such as transportation, hospitals, communication, lighting, power, water, and sewerage systems. They must also provide work and dwellings for people, as well as places for them to gather and enjoy themselves. Despite these shared features, no two cities are the same. Some have long histories and, thus, have old buildings. Others have grown recently and have mostly modern structures. Cities are built in different landscapes, from the coast to the mountains. Also, the different ways that people live make each city unique.

Dubai, United Arab Emirates

Since 1970, Dubai's population has grown rapidly from 183,000 to 1.5 million. Wealth from selling oil has been used to transform the city into an international center for trade, banking, and tourism. In 2010, Sheikh Mohammed, Dubai's ruler, opened Burj Khalifa, the world's tallest skyscraper.

Up and Down

Cities are crowded places where space is invaluable. Multi-layered living allows more people to fit in. Skyscrapers are tall buildings with many floors. Stores, offices, and homes can be located in skyscrapers instead of being spread out over the landscape. To save even more space in cities, parking garages, sewerage lines, and even train lines are located under the ground.

Store
In cities, many stores are located on street level. There they can be reached easily and passersby can see what is for sale in windows.

Parking Garage
There are rarely enough street parking spaces available for all the cars that people in a city use. Extra parking is provided in underground parking garages.

Rooftop garden
Many skyscrapers have flat roofs. These areas can be made into small, green spaces for people who live and work in the buildings.

City innovations

In 1863, the first underground rail system was opened in London. In 1884, the first ten-story skyscraper was built in Chicago, Illinois. Without these sorts of innovations, most cities could not support their millions of inhabitants and workers.

Apartment
Living right in the center of the city in an apartment can be very convenient for getting to work. There are also often wonderful views.

Office
Many businesses use office space in city skyscrapers. The central location makes it easy for companies to do business with each other.

Fly-over
As a city's population grows, so does its traffic. New roads are sometimes built on pylons that carry cars over existing buildings and streets.

Pipe
Pipes in cities are usually located under the ground. They carry water to and sewerage away from buildings. Workmen must dig down to repair them.

Train station
Some train lines run through tunnels in the central parts of many cities. People reach the underground station by traveling down escalators.

All Together

Cities bring many people together. City governments pool citizens' resources by collecting taxes and fees. The bigger and wealthier a city's population, the more funds that can be raised. Some of these funds are used to provide special places where people can gather and enrich their lives. Private businesses also open large attractions because they know they will draw in many visitors.

Exhibitions

Galleries and museums display works of art or historical objects. In Paris, the Louvre holds one of the world's great art collections. Each year more than 8.3 million people visit the gallery.

Places of worship

Many cities have large temples, mosques, or churches. These buildings are often imposing and awe-inspiring, and people can come together there to worship and celebrate religious occasions.

Monuments

Monuments can give cities special identities. The Statue of Liberty, erected in 1886, is one of the first things that comes to mind when people think about New York City.

Public places

Places that everyone can go to are one of the things that make living in cities special. Many cities have spectacular aquariums, zoos, botanical gardens, libraries, art galleries, museums, and places of worship for their citizens and visitors to use.

Amusement parks
People can let their hair down at amusement parks and enjoy live shows and rides. Disneyland in Hong Kong is on a small island beside the city.

Shopping heaven
Shopping is a major part of city life. Venues range from elegant department stores to busy markets, such as the Grand Bazaar in Istanbul, Turkey.

Fun in the City

There is always something going on in a city for citizens and tourists to enjoy. Many attractions—restaurants, shopping, plays, and movies—are available all year round. Other attractions are special events that might happen once a year, such as festivals or sporting events. Sometimes cities might even hold international events, such as the Olympic Games.

Sydney Opera House
Concerts, operas, and plays are performed in the Sydney Opera House. Rock concerts are held outside on the forecourt. In 2009, the building itself became part of a light show.

On parade
Many cities hold street parades. In New York City, a department store called Macy's has supported the Thanksgiving Day Parade since 1924.

Sporting events
Every four years, a city is chosen to host the Olympic Games. In 2008, they were held in the Chinese capital, Beijing.

Keeping Cities Clean

With so many people living together, one of the biggest challenges facing cities is keeping clean. Trash must be collected or it piles up, creating bad odors and attracting pests. Loud noise needs to be controlled so people can rest. Diseases are carried in polluted water, so sewage must be treated. If noise and air pollution, human waste, and trash are not dealt with, cities become unhealthy.

Pick it up!
Community trash collection programs, such as Clean Up Australia Day, help people become aware of litter. Many cities use recycling programs to reduce waste. If items such as bottles, cans, and paper are recycled, fewer of them end up in the environment.

Breathe in
Large numbers of factories and motor vehicles in cities cause air pollution. This can trigger allergies, asthma attacks, and other health problems. To reduce air pollution, some cities have penalties for heavy polluters, and commuters are encouraged to leave their cars at home.

Collecting trash
Huge amounts of trash are created in cities every day. It has to be collected or it would soon fill the streets. Street cleaners collect trash that has been dropped. Special trucks take trash to dumping stations away from residential areas.

Getting Around

Cities are vast, crowded places. People have to get from one location to another. They may live in one area but work in another. They may have to buy food and carry it home. They may have to go to a hospital, to a sports game, or to visit a friend. There are many ways to travel around in cities.

Ferry
The city of Sydney in Australia has grown up around a harbor. People living in harborside areas often use ferries.

Train
In Tokyo, Japan, millions of people use the clean and efficient rail services each day.

Bus
London's red buses are famous. Today, cleaner buses using hydrogen-powered electric engines are being introduced.

Public Transportation

Public transportation can carry large numbers of people using fewer vehicles. This saves fuel and reduces traffic congestion. If you travel by public transportation, you also do not have to worry about taking care of a car or finding a parking space.

Tram
In Hong Kong, 90 percent of journeys are on public transportation, usually on a tram known as a "Ding Ding."

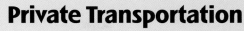

Private Transportation

Private transportation is convenient. If you have your own bicycle, car, or boat, you can travel wherever and whenever you like. You can use your own vehicle to carry your shopping, your pets, and even large items such as furniture.

Boat
On the outskirts of Bangkok, in Thailand, people live on canals. They travel in small boats.

Car
In Los Angeles, California, a larger percentage of people own cars than in any other city. Freeways carry heavy traffic.

Motorbike
As the city of Hanoi, in Vietnam has grown wealthier, faster motorbikes have replaced bicycles. Pollution has increased.

Bicycle
In the center of Amsterdam in the Netherlands, more people make trips on bicycles than in cars.

Wild in the City

People in cities need places to relax in a natural environment. Central Park in New York City is one of the world's most famous parks. There are many nonhuman park residents. Some of them, like raccoons and squirrels, live there all year. Others, including birds, pass on their seasonal migration. Human visitors to the park enjoy watching the wildlife.

Raccoon
The raccoon is nocturnal. During the day, it sleeps in tree hollows. It eats nuts, berries, insects, eggs, frogs, and human leftovers, such as pizza and bread.

Great blue heron
The great blue heron can be seen wading in the park's lakes. It eats small fish and aquatic insects and has been known to take snapping turtles.

Snapping turtle
The snapping turtle lives in lakes and ponds, digging holes for its eggs in sandy banks. It hunts small animals, such as insects and frogs.

Red-tailed hawk
The red-tailed hawk adapts well to city life. It feeds on small mammals, such as rats and squirrels, and nests on buildings by the park.

Eastern screech owl
The Eastern screech owl was once common in New York City but had almost disappeared by the 1960s. A program to reintroduce it began in the 1990s.

Eastern gray squirrel
The Eastern gray squirrel inhabits the park all year long and does not hibernate in winter. It eats nuts, seeds, and bark and makes nests in trees.

Brown rat
To avoid attracting rats, the park is kept as clean as possible. Poison is rarely used because hawks or owls might die from eating a poisoned rat.

Mallard duck
The mallard usually eats aquatic plants but is also fed by visitors. It lives in the park all year long, delighting visitors with its ducklings.

That's Amazing!
Central Park was founded in 1853 on 700 acres (283 ha) of rocky, swampy land. It was reshaped and thousands of trees were planted. In 1863, the park was extended to 843 acres (341 ha).

Slum dwellers

Cities in developing countries are growing very fast, forcing many people to live in slum areas with no services. Here, the poorest people pick over the city dumps to find things they can use or sell to earn money.

Rich and Poor

Wealthier people can afford to pay for the best a city has to offer. Poorer citizens, however, may not be able to pay for these things. In many cities, people from the countryside arrive every day to find jobs or gain access to education. Sometimes, the number of people arriving outstrips a government's ability to provide services, such as roads and sewerage systems.

Cities apart

Rio de Janeiro's richer occupants live near the beaches and lagoons or in the older, picturesque parts of the city. The poor live on the hillsides in shacks made of scrap metal and cardboard.

A wealthy person's home in Rio de Janeiro

A slum area in the hills of Rio de Janeiro

NO HOME TO GO TO

A homeless person is someone with no regular dwelling in which to sleep. In 2005, there were estimated to be 100 million homeless people worldwide. Many lived in cities. In 2009, there were 39,000 homeless people in New York City. Nearly half were children.

You Decide

Cities today face many challenges. The world's population is growing and cities are expected to keep growing too. At the same time, the world's wilderness areas, energy supplies, and clean water resources are shrinking. Important decisions must be made about many issues cities have to deal with, now and in the future.

HERITAGE

New buildings can be made to fit modern needs. However, we do not want all our buildings to be new or we will lose our heritage. Should old buildings be replaced with new ones?

Historical   Modern

ENERGY

Solar energy

With the world's cities needing ever more energy and some fuels running low, what can be done to supply it? Burning some fuels also harms the environment. Which kinds of fuels can give cities clean, safe, and affordable energy?

Power station

TRANSPORTATION

Should cities have more public transportation or more roads for cars? Private vehicles are convenient but use a lot of fuel and cause traffic jams. Public transportation uses less fuel and fewer vehicles are needed.

Private   Public

HOUSING

Building houses on blocks of land takes up a lot of space. On the other hand, apartment living can be cramped. Should people live in apartment buildings with parks nearby or spread out in suburbs?

Single-family   Apartment
homes   buildings

TRASH

Should cities recycle their trash or take it to dumps? Dumps need large areas of land and release harmful methane gas into the atmosphere. Recycling saves resources but requires complicated collecting systems.

Dump site   Recycling plant

What Do You Remember?

Try this quiz to see how much you can remember about cities.

1 Which city has trams that locals call "Ding Dings?"

2 What is the Burj Khalifa and in which city does it stand?

3 In 1348, what caused the population of London to shrink by half?

4 The Louvre, one of the world's great art galleries, is in which city?

5 Which ancient city went into decline after it was struck by an earthquake?

6 Which city hosted the Olympic Games in 2008?

7 In which year was the Statue of Liberty erected in New York City?

8 How many homeless people were there estimated to be in 2005?

Answers: 1 Hong Kong **2** World's tallest building; Dubai **3** The Black Death **4** Paris **5** Knossos **6** Beijing, China **7** 1886 **8** 100 million

Glossary

citizen (SIH-tih-zen)
Someone who lives in a city or town and has the right to use its services.

commuter
(kuh-MYOO-ter) A person who regularly travels some distance to and from work by car, train, bus, or other means of transportation.

congestion (kun-JES-chun)
The act of becoming overcrowded and blocked. Traffic congestion causes roads to become blocked.

efficient (ih-FIH-shent)
Able to do something well and on time, such as deliver passengers to their destination.

forecourt (FOHR-kohrt)
A court or open area in front of a building.

heritage (HER-uh-tij)
What is passed on to us by previous generations, such as buildings made by people of our grandparents' time.

hibernate (HY-bur-nayt)
To go into a sleeplike state in winter. Hibernating animals live off their body fat and do not eat.

infrastructure
(IN-freh-struk-chur)
The public works and buildings of a city or country used to provide services, such as the tracks and trains of a rail service.

innovations
(ih-nuh-VAY-shunz)
New and different things that are introduced to make improvements.

irrigation
(ih-rih-GAY-shun) A system of channels or pipes that carries water to land where crops are being grown.

landscapes (LAND-skayps)
The shape, appearance, and features of given areas of land, for example, coastal or mountainous landscapes.

Mesoamerica
(meh-soh-uh-MER-ih-kuh)
An area that includes Mexico and Central America, occupied in ancient times by people such as the Maya and Olmec.

metropolitan
(meh-truh-PAH-lih-ten)
Belonging to or relating to a major city.

migration
(my-GRAY-shun) The act of moving from one place to another, sometimes as a group.

picturesque
(pik-chuh-RESK) Charming and pleasing in appearance.

political (puh-LIH-tih-kul)
Having to do with governments and how a city or country is run.

population
(pop-yoo-LAY-shun) All the people living in a place, such as a city or country.

residential
(reh-zih-DEN-shul) Relating to somewhere that people live, rather than where they work or enjoy entertainment.

settlements
(SEH-tul-ments) Places where people live permanently, such as villages, towns, or cities.

sewerage (SOO-eh-rij)
A system of sewer pipes and pumps that carry sewage, which is human waste mixed with water.

Index

Websites

Due to the changing nature of Internet links, PowerKids Press has developed an online list of websites related to the subject of this book. This site is updated regularly. Please use this link to access the list: www.powerkidslinks.com/disc/urban/